DAYS OF DECISION

Churchill and the Battle of Britain

Heinemann
LIBRARY
Chicago, Illinois

Nicola Barber

© 2014 Heinemann Library
an imprint of Capstone Global Library, LLC
Chicago, Illinois

Visit our web site at www.heinemannraintree.com

Edited by Andrew Farrow, Adrian Vigliano, and Mark
Friedman
Designed by Cynthia Della-Rovere
Original illustrations © Capstone Global Library Ltd.
Illustrated by H L Studios and Cynthia Della-Rovere
Picture research by Elizabeth Alexander
Production by Sophia Argyris

Originated by Capstone Global Library Ltd
Printed in China by RR Donnelley South China

17 16 15 14 13
10 9 8 7 6 5 4 3 2 1

Library of Congress Cataloging-in-Publication Data
Barber, Nicola.

  Churchill and the Battle of Britain / Nicola Barber.

    pages cm.—(Days of decision)

  Includes bibliographical references and index.

  ISBN 978-1-4329-7634-7 (hb)—ISBN 978-1-4329-7641-5
(pb) 1. Britain, Battle of, Great Britain, 1940—Juvenile
literature. 2. Churchill, Winston, 1874-1965—Military
leadership—Juvenile literature. 3. World War, 1939-1945—
Great Britain—Juvenile literature. I. Title.

  D756.5.B7B35 2013

  940.54'211—dc23   2012041488

Acknowledgments
The author and publishers are grateful to the following for
permission to reproduce copyright material: ©Photoshot p.
6 (Eur); Alamy pp. 40, 46 (©INTERFOTO); Corbis pp. 18, 29
(©Hulton-Deutsch Collection), 21 (©Bettmann); Gamma-
Keystone via Getty Images pp. 33, 44, 48 (Keystone-France);
Getty Images pp. 5, 43 (Fox Photos/Hulton Archive), 4,
23 (Central Press/Hulton Archive), 12, 39 (Paul Popper/
Popperfoto), 24, 27 (Hulton Archive), 31 (Keystone/Hulton
Archive), 41 (Reg Speller/Fox Photos/Hulton Archive), 51
(Hugo Jaeger/Timepix/Time Life Pictures), 52, imprint (AFP);
©IWM p. 16; Photoshot p. 37 (©UPPA); Press Association
Images pp. 8 (Sport and General/S&G Barratts/Empics
Archive), 14, 30 (PA Archive), 26 (AP).

Background and design features reproduced with the
permission of Shutterstock (©Picsfive, ©Petrov Stanislav,
©Zastolskiy Victor, ©design36, ©a454).

Cover photograph of Winston Churchill in 1945 reproduced
with the permission of Alamy (©Pictorial Press Ltd); Cover
photograph of a squadron of British fighters in flight
reproduced with the permission of Corbis (©Bettmann).

We would like to thank Dr. John Allen Williams for his
invaluable help in the preparation of this book.

Contents

Some words are printed in **bold**, like this. You can find out what they mean by looking in the glossary on page 59.

A Decisive Day

It is September 15, 1940. As wave after wave of German **bombers** fly toward southern England, UK **Prime Minister** Winston Churchill, with his trademark cigar clamped between his teeth, makes his way to Royal Air Force (RAF) headquarters in London. There, he is met by Air Vice-Marshal Keith Park, the man responsible for the RAF **squadrons** defending London and the southeast of England from air attack.

September 14, 1940: At the height of the Battle of Britain, Hurricane fighter planes take off from an airfield in the south of the UK to defend against German attacks.

Deep underground in the operations room, Churchill and Park watch as counters on a large tabletop map track the progress of the German attacks. As each squadron of RAF fighters takes off to intercept the enemy, a light on a board comes on to show that the planes are airborne.

Early in the afternoon, as the lights flash on one by one, Churchill turns to Park. "What reserves have we got?" he asks. "There are none," replies Park. Every single squadron is in the air, battling to defend the United Kingdom.[1] Churchill and Park both know that this is a decisive moment in the defense of the United Kingdom against a possible German invasion. In order to win, the Germans need to destroy the RAF. This is now a battle for survival.

Battle of Britain Day

Since the end of World War II, September 15 has been commemorated in the United Kingdom as Battle of Britain Day, the day when the RAF fighters managed to hold out against the German bombers. The battle was by no means over, but many people consider this day to mark a crucial turning point in the Battle of Britain. Yet for Churchill, it was one of many such crucial moments, both in the past and yet to come.

The man for the moment?

Churchill had become prime minister of the United Kingdom in May 1940. At the time, many powerful people had questioned some of his past decisions and were less than enthusiastic about giving him this role. But as the German Army stormed across Europe and overwhelmed France, the majority of people came to believe that Churchill was the right man for the moment. A U.S. journalist for the *Philadelphia Inquirer* wrote of Churchill's first speech as prime minister: "He proved himself an honest man as well as a man of action. Britain has reason to be enheartened by his... bluntness and his courage."[2]

So, what were the qualities that made Churchill such an inspirational war leader and helped to win the Battle of Britain? And what crucial decisions did Churchill make as the United Kingdom struggled to come to terms with the disastrous fall of France in 1940, as well as the threat of imminent German invasion?

A crowd follows Winston Churchill (center) as he makes one of his frequent visits to inspect bomb damage after German raids in London.

Decisive words: Churchill alone

"Everything depended on him and him alone. Only he had the power to make the nation believe that it could win."[3]

Edward Bridges, cabinet secretary, writing about Winston Churchill between 1940 and 1942

Who Was Winston Churchill?

Winston Leonard Spencer Churchill was born on November 30, 1874, at Blenheim Palace, near Oxford, England. His father, Lord Randolph Churchill, was the youngest son of the 7th Duke of Marlborough, which meant that Churchill was descended from one of the United Kingdom's most famous generals, John Churchill (1650–1722), 1st Duke of Marlborough. His mother, Jennie Jerome, was the daughter of a wealthy banker from New York.

Blenheim Palace was a gift from Queen Anne and the nation to John Churchill, in thanks for his part in the victory at the Battle of Blenheim in 1704. Winston Churchill was born there in 1874.

As was usual for the time, Winston Churchill was raised mostly by a much-loved nanny, Mrs. Everest, and was then sent to boarding school at the age of seven. He did not shine academically at Harrow School, and he later wrote of his time there: "I was on the whole considerably discouraged by my school days."[1] He did, however, manage (on the third attempt) to pass the exams to enter the Royal Military Academy at Sandhurst, the place where all officers in the British Army are trained. Churchill graduated in 1894, taking up a post as a cavalry officer (a soldier on horseback) the following year.

Churchill may have come from a grand and wealthy family but, largely due to the huge costs of running and maintaining Blenheim Palace, his family was constantly short of money.

After his father's death in 1895, Churchill received an allowance from his mother, in addition to his army pay. But it was never enough to allow him to live him in the style he considered appropriate. This may have been one reason why he began to take on work as a war correspondent for various newspapers, often alongside his army duties. Reporting from Cuba in 1895, he came under fire for the first time, on his 21st birthday. He also acquired his lifelong love of Cuban cigars.[2]

Start of a political career

Even as he began his army career, Churchill was thinking about the possibilities beyond it. His father had been active in UK politics as a member of **Parliament** (MP) for the **Conservative Party**—a political party that emphasized the traditional values of stability and continuity. Churchill was therefore already well connected in the world of politics, and after his father's death, he relied on his mother to promote his cause.

In 1899, Churchill decided to leave the army and pursue a political career. His first attempt to become a member of parliament ended in failure. But in the **general election** of 1900, he succeeded in his bid to be Conservative MP for Oldham, in the northwest of England.

Churchill quickly made his mark in politics. As an elected MP, he entered the House of Commons (the lower chamber of Parliament). His first speech in the Commons was about the situation in southern Africa, and he called for the fair treatment of the defeated Boers.[3]

Escaped prisoner

In 1899, Churchill worked as a correspondent to report on the war in southern Africa between the British and the **Boers** of the South African Republic and the Orange Free State. In an episode of high drama, he showed great bravery in helping to rescue an armored train that was ambushed by the Boers. He was taken prisoner, but a month later he managed to escape by scrambling over the outer wall of the prison. After his safe return, Churchill found that he had become a hero. His newfound fame played a major part in his election as an MP in 1900.[4]

It was Churchill's support for the policy of **free trade** that caused the first major upheaval of his political career. Some members of the Conservative Party, including **Colonial** Secretary Joseph Chamberlain, wanted to introduce tariffs (taxes) on food and other goods that were imported into the United Kingdom. They argued that such tariffs would protect UK manufacturing and businesses from what they considered "unfair" competition from abroad. Churchill and other supporters of free trade disagreed.

It was over this issue that Churchill made the decision, in May 1904, to leave the Conservatives and join the opposition **Liberal Party**. This was a bold move, and soon Churchill was speaking out against his former colleagues. The issue of free trade eventually caused the Conservative prime minister to resign, and there was a general election in 1906. When the Liberals won, Churchill accepted a post dealing with colonial matters in the new government.

Class traitor?

In the following years, Churchill played a major role in the Liberal government, working at the Board of Trade (the committee responsible for the country's economic life). Then, in 1910, he became home secretary, meaning he was in charge of the Home

Winston Churchill and his wife, Clementine, during the early days of their marriage.

Office, with responsibility for security, the police, immigration, and more. He helped to introduce many anti-poverty laws and was involved in prison reform.

Churchill also backed proposals to curb the power of the House of Lords, the unelected upper chamber of Parliament made up of lords (who inherit their titles) as well as bishops of the Church of England. Churchill's support for this issue did not please many Conservatives. They considered Churchill not only to be a traitor to the Conservative Party, but also to the class of wealthy landowners into which he had been born. Nevertheless, Churchill's rise to a glittering political career seemed set.[5]

First lord of the Admiralty

In 1911, Churchill became **first lord of the Admiralty**, the political head of the Royal Navy (as opposed to the professional head of the navy). He took charge at a time when the supremacy of the Royal Navy was being challenged by steadily increasing German naval power. Since the turn of the century, the two nations had been engaged in an arms race to build up their navies. In 1906, the British had built the Dreadnought, a battleship that was faster and armed with bigger guns than any ship previously built. In his new post, Churchill argued successfully for further spending on the navy and ensured that when war broke out in 1914, the Royal Navy was ready for action.

Clementine, Baroness Spencer-Churchill 1885–1977

Born: London, United Kingdom

Role: Wife of Winston Churchill and mother of their five children: Diana, Randolph, Sarah, Marigold, and Mary[6]

Winston Churchill first met Clementine Hozier briefly in 1904, but when they met again in 1908, he fell in love. They married in the same year, and, throughout her life, Clementine devoted herself to Winston.[7]

Did you know? Winston and Clemmie, as he called her, wrote to each other every day of their married lives—often even if they were in the same house. Winston's pet name for his wife was "cat"; her name for him was "pug."[8]

Gallipoli and After

In August 1914, World War I (1914–1918) was breaking out. German armies marched across **neutral** Belgium to invade France. In response, the French Army attacked the French–German border.

Meanwhile, the United Kingdom was drawn into the war by a **treaty** that committed the United Kingdom to defend Belgium. So, the United Kingdom shipped the first troops of the **British Expeditionary Force (BEF)** across the English Channel. By the end of 1914, the **Allies** (the British Empire and France) and the Germans had reached a standstill along a line of defensive trench systems, known as the Western Front, that stretched across Europe from the English Channel to the border with Switzerland.

War at sea

In 1914, neither the United Kingdom nor Germany wanted a direct confrontation at sea, because neither side wanted to see their ships destroyed in battle. One of the main aims of the Royal Navy was to protect vital trade routes into the United Kingdom. But German fleets in the Indian and Pacific oceans soon attacked UK shipping.

Closer to home, the Royal Navy succeeded in sinking three German ships in the North Sea on August 28. In September, **torpedoes** fired from a German **U-boat** sank three British cruisers.

At the beginning of 1915, Churchill put forward a new strategy. He wanted to find a way to break the deadlock on the Western Front—

World War I: Key facts

In World War I, on one side were the Central Powers, made up of Germany, Austria-Hungary, and the **Ottoman Empire** (Turkey). On the other side were the Allies, made up of France, the British Empire, Russia, Italy, Japan, and the United States (from 1917). The following timeline lists the major events in the war in 1914:

October 29	October 18–November 12	August 28
The Ottoman Empire enters the war on the side of the Central Powers.	The First Battle of Ypres ends with a stalemate (no winner), as both sides dig into trenches along the Western Front.	The naval battle of Heligoland Bight is fought.

The Dardanelles is a narrow strait that is about 37 miles long. It provides a route between the Mediterranean and the Black seas. The Gallipoli Peninsula forms the north side of this strait, while the mainland of Turkey forms the south side.

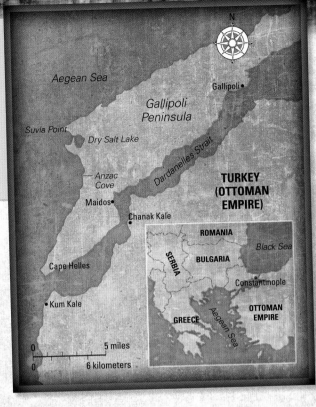

an alternative, as he put it, to "sending our troops to chew barbed wire in Flanders [Belgium]."[1]

Churchill proposed an attack against Turkey, one of Germany's weaker allies, far away from the main action. The Turks had entered the war on the side of the **Central Powers** in November 1914.

Churchill's plan was to send British ships through the Dardanelles (see the map). He believed that if the Royal Navy could take control there, and even threaten Constantinople (the Ottoman capital), Turkey might surrender. In addition, this strategy was designed to distract the attention of the Central Powers away from the Eastern Front, where the Russians were struggling against the German and Austrian-Hungarian armies.[2]

August 1	August 3	August 4
Germany declares war on Russia.	Germany declares war on France. The German Army invades Belgium.	The United Kingdom declares war on Germany. U.S. President Woodrow Wilson declares a U.S. policy of neutrality.

August 23	August 17	August 9-16	August 6 onward
Austria-Hungary invades Russian Poland (on the Eastern Front).	Russia invades East Prussia (on the Eastern Front).	The BEF lands in France.	The Battle of the Frontiers (on the Western Front) is fought.

The Royal Navy at Gallipoli

On February 19, 1915, British and French warships began a naval **bombardment** of Gallipoli. Although the bombardment knocked out some of the Turkish forts on shore, it could not reach forts that were further inland. The Turks had also laid minefields in the straits. These **mines** exploded if a ship hit them.

On March 18, the Allies tried to force their way through the straits with 18 French and three British battleships.[3] Three ships sank after they hit mines, and three more were seriously damaged.[4] Over 700 sailors lost their lives. Churchill had to admit that the Royal Navy could not do the job without a full-scale military operation to seize the Turkish forts. That way, the minefields could be cleared in safety.

Allied failure

After the loss of another battleship to a Turkish torpedo in May, the head of the Royal Navy, Lord Admiral John Fisher, resigned over disagreements with Churchill. A few days later, Churchill himself was removed from his post in the **Admiralty**, although he remained in the government.

Allied troops began to land on the Gallipoli peninsula in April, but they made very little progress and took huge **casualties**. By September, it was clear that no progress would be made without

Churchill championed the development of the tank as early as 1915. In 1917, as minister of munitions, Churchill threw his energies into the production of tanks, which played a major role on the Western Front in the Battle of Cambrai on November 20, 1917.

massive reinforcements that the Allies did not have. In November, the decision was made to end the operation, and by January 9, 1916, all Allied troops had been evacuated from the peninsula. Allied casualties for the whole campaign were around 265,000.[5]

The failure of the Gallipoli campaign was a massive blow to the Allies—and to Churchill in particular. Years later, after Churchill's death, his wife, Clementine, commented: "The Dardanelles haunted him [Churchill] for the rest of his life. He always believed in it. When he left the Admiralty he thought he was finished. I thought he would never get over the Dardanelles; I thought he would die of grief."[6] It certainly marked a moment of political failure in Churchill's career.

It was also disastrous for the Allies in terms of the number of men killed and injured. And although the Turks also suffered heavy casualties, their victory at Gallipoli stiffened their resolve to fight on.[7] In the United Kingdom, the resignation of Admiral Fisher in May 1915 forced the Liberals to reorganize and to form a **coalition government** with the Conservatives.[8]

Minister for munitions

In November 1915, Churchill left politics and returned to his army career, working as an officer in active service in France. But, despite fierce protests from the Conservatives, the Liberal prime minister, David Lloyd George, brought Churchill back to the government in 1917. Lloyd George appointed Churchill minister for munitions, meaning he was in charge of the equipment used for wars, such as weapons. In this role, Churchill was heavily involved in the development of the tank—an innovation that eventually helped to break the deadlock on the Western Front.

Between Two Wars

In late 1918, after the end of World War I, Lloyd George appointed Churchill as minister for war. Included in Churchill's new position was the responsibility for the Royal Air Force (RAF).

Churchill was already enthusiastic about military aircraft. During his time at the Admiralty in 1911, he had supported the establishment of the first naval flying school, which became the Royal Naval Air Service (RNAS) in 1914. In 1919, Churchill asked Hugh Trenchard to be the chief of staff of the RAF. Together, the two men laid the foundations for the organization and role of the RAF of the future.

Churchill (right) started flying lessons in 1913 but a few years later, after a crash that left him badly bruised, he gave up learning to fly before earning his certificate.

New technology

Aircraft had been used throughout World War I, although the technology was very new. At first, planes were mainly used as "eyes in the sky" for **reconnaissance** and to guide **artillery** bombardments. But Trenchard introduced a more aggressive strategy, in which pilots both fought other pilots and bombed the enemy on the ground.

From 1915 onward, there had been bombing raids on cities and other targets. German raids—such as the one on London in June 1917, that killed 162 people and injured over 400 more—made a big impression.[1] Many people, including Churchill, thought that if another war ever happened, it would be fought in the air, with massive bombing campaigns against major towns and cities.

Cost-cutting

World War I left the United Kingdom with massive debts. One of the government's first priorities was to reduce the size of the armed forces back to peacetime levels. As minister for war, it fell to Churchill to organize the process of **demobilizing** thousands of soldiers, sailors, and airmen and women. In a time of such severe economic hardship, there were many people who considered the RAF an expensive luxury that the country simply could not afford. But both Churchill and Trenchard fought hard for the continuation of the RAF.

Decisive words: Bombing capacity

In 1918, Churchill declared that, in the future, victory would belong to the side that:

"possessed the power to drop not five tons but five hundred tons of bombs each night on the cities and manufacturing establishments of its opponents."[2]

Hugh Montague Trenchard 1873-1956

Born: Taunton, United Kingdom

Role: RAF chief of staff

During World War I, Hugh Trenchard was commander of the Royal Flying Corps (RFC), which was part of the army. In April 1918, the RFC and RNAS were unified to form the RAF, with Trenchard as its chief of staff, although he resigned almost immediately. Churchill reappointed him in 1919, and Trenchard then set about creating new ranks and uniforms for the RAF, in addition to setting up training colleges. Trenchard fought hard for the RAF during a time of government spending cuts and against the competing claims of the other armed forces.

Did you know? As a young officer in the British Army, Trenchard was posted to India, where he played polo (a team sport played on horseback). In 1896, he played a match against a team that included another officer of almost exactly the same age named Winston Churchill.[3] This was their first meeting.

Policing the empire

In 1921, Churchill moved to a post in the Colonial Office. One of the legacies of World War I was that the United Kingdom now had direct responsibility for governing large areas of the Middle East, including Palestine and Mesopotamia, that had been part of the defeated Ottoman Empire.

From the moment he took up his post as colonial secretary, Churchill looked for ways to save money by reducing the number of troops in these regions. Churchill decided to use the RAF to "police" Mesopotamia and elsewhere, rather than keeping large numbers of troops on the ground. Experts quickly found that aircraft could patrol large areas much more quickly, effectively, and cheaply than soldiers on the ground. This strategy of using the RAF to control parts of the British Empire was known as Air Control, and it provided Trenchard with persuasive arguments to justify the continuing existence of the RAF.

This photo shows an RAF plane stationed in Egypt, during the Air Control years.

The 10-Year Rule

Trenchard also spoke of the need for an air force based at home. In 1923, Prime Minister Stanley Baldwin said that there should be a Home Defense Air Force sufficiently strong to protect the United

Kingdom against air attack. It was decided that the RAF needed 52 squadrons, including both bombers and fighters, for this role. But, due to government spending cuts through the 1920s and 1930s, this number of squadrons was never achieved.

It was Churchill himself, in charge of the nation's finances as **Chancellor of the Exchequer** from 1924 until 1929, who halted defense spending in the RAF and elsewhere. His policy was based on what was known as the 10-Year Rule. This was a guideline introduced in 1919 that assumed the United Kingdom would not be involved in a major war for the next 10 years, and that spending on the armed forces should be based on this assumption.

Churchill cuts the navy

The 10-Year Rule was part of an international commitment to a general reduction of all **armaments** after World War I. A conference held in Washington, DC in 1921–1922, led to an agreement on quotas (limits) for the number of battleships in the navies of the United Kingdom, the United States, Japan, France, and Italy.[6] In fact, the Royal Navy was hit particularly hard by Churchill's defense cuts, with consequences for a wide variety of industries such as shipbuilding and steel, in addition to manufacturers of guns, ammunition, and naval equipment.

Back to the Conservative Party

Churchill became Chancellor of the Exchequer in 1924, after two difficult years. In the general election of 1922, he had failed to be re-elected as a Liberal MP, after a miserable campaign when he was suddenly sick with appendicitis. He later wrote: "In the twinkling of an eye I found myself without an office, without a seat, without a party, and without an appendix."[4]

When the Liberal Party decided to side with the **Labour Party** government in January 1924, Churchill broke with the Liberals for good and decided to join the Conservatives once more. Churchill knew that switching sides for the second time would make many people question his motives and loyalty. He remarked: "Anyone can rat [betray], but it takes a certain amount of ingenuity to re-rat."[5]

Winston Churchill is carried from a nursing home on a stretcher after his appendicitis operation during the general election campaign in 1922.

Independence for India

The Conservatives lost the general election of 1929, and Churchill found himself out of office once again. The fact that he remained out of the government until 1939 was largely a result of his attitude to one of the major issues of the day—independence for India.

The movement for independence had been growing throughout the 1920s and 1930s, led by Mohandas Gandhi. Churchill vigorously opposed any kind of self-rule for India, which was a UK colony, arguing that it would herald the collapse of the British Empire. But he was proven wrong by the passing of the Government of India Act in 1935, which introduced some political reform without any of the dire consequences that Churchill feared. The act, however, failed to satisfy the demands of many Indians, and support for complete independence continued to grow in India.

The threat from Nazi Germany

Meanwhile, another issue of foreign policy was attracting Churchill's attention. In January 1933, Adolf Hitler had become chancellor of Germany. By July, Hitler's **Nazi Party** was the only permitted political party in Germany, as all other parties were banned. In 1934, Hitler's position as **dictator** became clear when he ordered the arrest and execution of many of his political enemies.

At the same time, the Nazis were expanding and rearming Germany's armed forces. In 1936, Hitler sent troops to occupy the Rhineland, an area to the west of the Rhine River. According to the terms of the Treaty of Versailles, an agreement signed after Germany lost World War I, this area was supposed to be controlled by the Allies. Hitler's action broke the terms of the treaty, but neither the United Kingdom nor France opposed Germany's aggression.

Decisive words: Churchill's warning

In a radio broadcast on November 15, 1934, Churchill said the following:

"When we look out upon the state of Europe and of the world and of the position of our own country as they are tonight, it seems to me that the next year or two years may contain a fateful turning point in our history. I am afraid that if you look intently at what is moving towards Great Britain, you will see that the only choice open is the old grim choice our forebears had to face, namely…whether we shall submit to the will of the stronger nation or whether we shall prepare to defend our rights, our liberties, and indeed, our lives."[8]

As the brutal and threatening nature of Hitler's regime (government) became increasingly apparent, it was Churchill who warned about the need to take the developments in Germany very seriously. But by now, he was distrusted by politicians from all sides and considered by many people to lack good judgment. His warnings were largely ignored. As historian Arthur Herman put it: "He [Churchill] had cried wolf for nearly five years, forecasting doom and destruction if the Government of India bill passed… When he forecast doom again, over Germany, few were inclined to believe him."[7] For a nation still traumatized by the horrors of World War I, there was also a great unwillingness even to consider the possibility of another war.

Rearmament

Alongside his warnings about Nazi Germany, Churchill urged the need for **rearmament**. A decade before, he had been busy cutting back the armed forces (see page 17), but now he saw very clearly the need to build them back up. Despite not having a government post, Churchill was still given access to official government reports, and he was even consulted on matters relating to the air force and rearmament.

Churchill concentrated particularly on the RAF, as he considered the threat from the German Air Force, the **Luftwaffe**, to be great. In a speech to the House of Commons in 1934, he warned of the effects of massive bombing raids on London, saying: "No one can doubt that a week or ten days' intensive bombing attack upon London would be a very serious matter indeed. One could hardly expect that less than 30,000 or 40,000 people would be killed or maimed."[9]

The Luftwaffe

The Treaty of Versailles, signed after World War I, forbade Germany from having an air force. But the Germans secretly built aircraft and trained pilots during the 1920s. (Many pilots learned to fly in glider clubs, which were permitted.) In 1935, Hitler ordered Hermann Goering, his loyal supporter and a leading member of the Nazi Party, to set up the Luftwaffe. By 1939, the Luftwaffe had expanded rapidly and was ready to support full-scale war.[12] Unlike the RAF, the Luftwaffe worked closely with the German Army and German Navy, and it was particularly effective in supporting troops on the ground, as would be seen during the **blitzkrieg** of 1939–1940 (see page 26).

Bomber or fighter?

Churchill argued for spending on the RAF, not only as a means of defense against the Luftwaffe, but also as a means of attack on Germany. He believed that "strategic bombing"—the bombing of targets such as railroads, ports, and industrial areas—would play a major role in any war.

Churchill was not alone in this belief. In 1932, Stanley Baldwin, a Conservative minister, told the House of Commons: "I think it is well for the man in the street to realize that there is no power on

Earth that can protect him from being bombed. Whatever people may tell him, the bomber will always get through."[10]

In the 1930s, the RAF developed long-range strategic bombers such as the Vickers Wellington. However, it was two new fighter planes that were to play the major role in the Battle of Britain. The first prototype Hurricane flew in 1935, and the Spitfire flew in 1936.[11]

December 1939: a squadron of British Spitfire fighter planes in flight. These were single-seater aircraft with machine guns mounted in the wings.

Early warning system

In 1936, the RAF was reorganized into four separate sections, or "commands": Fighter, Bomber, Coastal (for the protection of ships), and Training. The man who took charge of Fighter Command was Air Chief Marshal Hugh Dowding.

Dowding did not agree with Baldwin's assessment that "the bomber will always get through." He masterminded an early warning system that used a combination of **radar** and human observers, who reported back to his Fighter Command headquarters. The aim of this system was to enable fighter aircraft to intercept bombers before they reached their targets. This system would later prove vital in the Battle of Britain (see page 35).

German aggression

In 1938, Hitler sent German troops into Austria. On March 14, Hitler himself drove triumphantly into Vienna, the Austrian capital, to celebrate the Anschluss (unification) of Austria with Germany. The UK and French governments protested to Germany, but they took no other action. Hitler now had his sights set on Czechoslovakia and demanded that the Sudetenland, a region bordering Germany that was home to many German-speakers, be handed over to German control.

Appeasement

These actions led the UK prime minister, Neville Chamberlain, to fly to Munich, Germany, in September 1938 for a meeting with the German leader. In an effort to avoid war at all costs, Chamberlain helped bring about the Munich Agreement. In this agreement, Chamberlain adopted a policy called **appeasement**, which means giving concessions to an aggressive power in order to keep the peace. Together with representatives from France and Italy, Chamberlain agreed to allow Hitler to take over the Sudetenland, as long as the Germans went no further.

Chamberlain's policy was met with international approval. From the United States, President Franklin D. Roosevelt sent a telegram with the simple message: "Good man." Chamberlain returned to the United Kingdom a hero, greeted by jubilant

Neville Chamberlain 1896–1940
Born: Birmingham, United Kingdom

Role: Conservative UK prime minister, 1937–1940

Like many people who had lived through World War I, Neville Chamberlain was determined to prevent another war if at all possible. He did, however, support rearmament when the threat from Nazi Germany became apparent in the 1930s, and he particularly urged the strengthening of the RAF. After the failure of the Munich Agreement, Chamberlain declared war on Germany in September 1939. He resigned in May 1940, as Hitler's armies invaded the Netherlands, Belgium, and France. He died a few months later.

Did you know? In recognition of his efforts to prevent the outbreak of widespread war in Europe in 1938, Chamberlain was nominated for the Nobel Peace Prize in the following year.[15] In fact, the prize was not awarded to anyone in 1939.

Neville Chamberlain proclaims "peace for our time" on his return from Munich after meeting with Adolf Hitler in September 1938.

crowds. He addressed them with the words: "I believe it is peace for our time... Now I recommend you go home, and sleep quietly in your beds."[13]

Churchill was one of the few people who spoke out against the Munich Agreement, which was soon shown to be worthless. In a speech in June 1938, he said: "The idea that dictators can be appeased by kind words and minor concessions is doomed to disappointment... The dictator countries are prepared night and day to advance their ambitions if possible by peace, if necessary by war. I am under the impression that we and other countries stand in great danger."[14]

For Prime Minster Chamberlain and many others, however, the prospect of war was too appalling, and peace at almost any price remained their aim.

Decisive words: "All is over"

These powerful words are from the speech Churchill gave to the House of Commons after the Munich Agreement of 1938. After this speech, Churchill found himself in danger of losing his seat as an MP because of the unpopularity of his "warmongering" views:

"I will, therefore, begin by saying the most unpopular and most unwelcome thing. I will begin by saying what everybody would like to ignore or forget but which must nevertheless be stated, namely, that we have sustained a total and unmitigated defeat... All is over. Silent, mournful, abandoned, broken, Czechoslovakia recedes into the darkness."[16]

Outbreak of War

From 1929 to 1939, Churchill was largely out of government (although he remained an MP), and, for the most part, his views were largely ignored. But the outbreak of World War II led to an extraordinary and rapid turnaround in Churchill's fortunes.

"Winston is back"

As Churchill had predicted, hopes for peace in Europe were soon shattered. On November 9, 1938, Nazi thugs targeted Jewish communities in German and Austrian towns and cities, burning down synagogues (Jewish houses of worship) and smashing store windows. Many Jews were arrested or killed in these attacks. Then, in March 1939, Hitler took control of Czechoslovakia and threatened Poland.

On September 1, the Nazis invaded Poland. Both the United Kingdom and France had promised to help Poland in the event of an unprovoked attack. So, on September 3, the United Kingdom and France declared war on Germany. That same day, Chamberlain appointed Churchill back to his old post at the Admiralty. According to Churchill's memoirs, the Admiralty sent out a signal (message) to all ships of the Royal Navy, saying: "Winston is back."[1]

Battle rages in the Norwegian port of Narvik, in 1940. Narvik was important for the export of iron ore because its waters remained free of ice throughout the winter.

"Phoney war"

A period followed that is known as the "phoney war"—a time when the Allies had no land-based offensive against the Germans, although there was considerable action at sea. Within hours of the declaration of war, a German torpedo sunk a UK passenger ship, the SS *Athenia*, and on September 4, the Allies began a naval blockade of Germany, meaning they tried to prevent food and raw materials from getting through.

In December, Churchill noted that Germany was importing much-needed supplies of iron ore from Norway and Sweden, which were both neutral countries. He argued that the seas around Norway should be mined, to prevent these shipments from getting through. In fact, the action went further, with UK troops landing in Norway in April 1940. The result was disastrous: Hitler took the opportunity to invade and occupy both Denmark and Norway, and the UK troops were forced to retreat.

Echoes of Gallipoli

For Churchill, the failure of this action had echoes of the disastrous Gallipoli campaign in World War I. After Gallipoli, his reputation had been seriously damaged. But in May 1940, it was Prime Minister Chamberlain who was forced to resign over the action in Norway.

Decisive words: Blood, toil, tears, and sweat

Churchill made his first speech as prime minister to the House of Commons on May 13, 1940. He said:

"I have nothing to offer but blood, toil, tears, and sweat… We have before us many, many long months of struggle and of suffering. You ask, what is our policy? I can say: It is to wage war, by sea, land, and air, with all our might and with all the strength that God can give us… You ask, what is our aim? I can answer in one word: It is victory, victory at all costs, victory in spite of all terror…for without victory, there is no survival."[4]

The choice to succeed Chamberlain was between Churchill and Foreign Secretary Lord Halifax. Halifax had the support of most of the Conservative Party and King George VI, but he recognized that he was not suited to be a wartime prime minister—he said that the thought left him "with a bad stomach-ache."[2]

Instead, on May 10, 1940, Churchill became prime minister. His initial reaction was one of relief. He later wrote: "At last I had the authority to give directions over the whole scene. I felt as if I were walking with destiny, and that all my past life had been but a preparation for this hour and this trial."[3]

25

Blitzkrieg

As he took office, Churchill is said to have commented about the British public: "Poor people. They trust me, and I can give them nothing but disaster for quite a long time."[5] The events of the following few weeks were, indeed, catastrophic, as Germany invaded Belgium, the Netherlands, Luxembourg, and France. The Germans used blitzkrieg ("lightning war") tactics—a concentration of fast-moving tanks and motorized artillery followed by troops, all well supported by air power. As a result, they overwhelmed the opposition with terrifying speed.

September 6, 1939: German armored tanks, flanked by riders on motorcycles, move through Poland.

The BEF and RAF

After the declaration of war in September 1939, the United Kingdom had dispatched the British Expeditionary Force (BEF) to France, in preparation for a German attack. The BEF had been formed in 1908, but it was a race against time to recruit enough troops and to equip them. At the outbreak of war, Britain had 10 infantry (foot soldier) divisions, while Germany had 100.[6]

The RAF sent planes for reconnaissance work, just as it had in World War I, in addition to bombers and fighters. However, there was still little cooperation between air and ground forces, and the RAF found itself unable to cope with the strength of the Luftwaffe. In the battle fought over France from mid-May to early June 1940, the RAF lost nearly 1,000 aircraft, 320 pilots were killed, and another 115 pilots were captured.[7]

Dilemma

As the German blitzkrieg overtook France, Churchill was faced with some extraordinarily difficult decisions. If France collapsed, the United Kingdom was effectively left alone to stand against the Nazi threat. The French prime minister, Paul Reynaud, urgently wanted the United Kingdom to send more troops, but this was impossible, given the state of the BEF. Reynaud also asked for more aircraft, to support the ground forces. Churchill's dilemma was: Should he throw everything into preventing a French defeat, or should he protect the United Kingdom's ability to fight on alone?

Air Chief Marshal Hugh Dowding, in charge of Fighter Command, did not want to sacrifice his precious fighter squadrons in return for no gain on the battlefields of France. But Churchill had promised Reynaud that the United Kingdom would provide more air power. At a meeting between Dowding and Churchill on May 15, 1940, Dowding expressed his concerns about the loss of aircraft and pilots in France. The next day, Dowding reinforced his views in a 10-point letter to the **Air Ministry** (see the box below).

In the end, a compromise solution was agreed upon, with six more squadrons providing cover over northern France, from where they could return to the safety of English bases each night.

Air Chief Marshal Hugh Dowding remained in charge of RAF Fighter Command during the Battle of Britain.

Decisive words: Desperate attempts

In his letter on May 16, 1940, Dowding stated his reasons for opposing Churchill's promise to send more aircraft to France, saying, in part:

"I believe that if an adequate fighter force is kept in this country…we should be able to carry on the war single-handed for some time. But if the Home Defence Force is drained away in desperate attempts to remedy the situation in France, defeat in France will involve the final, complete, and irremediable defeat of this country."[8]

The Battle for France

From the moment Churchill became prime minister, he had tried his best to encourage the French to stand firmly against the German armies that were advancing on France. In total, he visited France six times in May and June 1940 to talk with members of the French government.[9] It was Churchill's desperation to support France that led him to promise more air squadrons, against the advice of Dowding. He wanted to give the French Army a last chance to "rally its bravery and strength."[10]

But as the situation in France became increasingly desperate, it was clear that the BEF and the French Army could not hold out against the German forces. On May 26, Churchill authorized the decision to bring as many troops as possible back to England. The only port not under German control was Dunkirk, on the French coast. The evacuation from Dunkirk began on May 26 (see the box below).

Desperate measures

While the evacuation from Dunkirk was underway, Churchill was exploring all his options with his war cabinet. Halifax, appointed by Churchill to be foreign secretary, was prepared to consider peace negotiations with Hitler. Churchill argued fiercely against him and eventually won the debate.

Operation Dynamo

The evacuation of Dunkirk, code-named Operation Dynamo, was a desperate rescue attempt. At first, Churchill feared that only 50,000 troops would be saved. But in the end, around 335,000 UK, French, and Belgian troops were shipped back to the English coast, in a fleet of every type of boat or ship that could cross to France and back.[12]

The whole operation was only possible because Hitler had halted the German blitzkrieg outside Dunkirk for rest and repairs. It was, however, a race against time to evacuate the troops before the German advance resumed, and a huge amount of valuable equipment was abandoned in the process. The RAF played a major part in the skies above Dunkirk, as its fighters protected the soldiers on the beaches below from the Luftwaffe. Churchill commented: "There was a victory inside this deliverance, which should be noted. It was gained by the Air Force."[13]

Decisive words: "We shall fight on the beaches..."

Churchill knew the danger of viewing Dunkirk as a "victory," and in a speech to the House of Commons on June 4, he warned that "wars are not won by evacuations." In the stirring conclusion to this speech, he stated his resolve to fight on, saying:

"We shall go on to the end, we shall fight in France, we shall fight on the seas and oceans, we shall fight with growing confidence and growing strength in the air, we shall defend our Island, whatever the cost may be, we shall fight on the beaches, we shall fight on the landing grounds, we shall fight in the fields and in the streets, we shall fight in the hills; we shall never surrender."[14]

But as a new prime minister, Churchill knew that he did not yet have the complete trust or backing of many of his Conservative colleagues. He continued to cling to the hope that France would not come under German control, and he went as far as proposing that France and the United Kingdom should join to form one united state. But even as this plan was under discussion, the French were asking the Germans for an **armistice**.[11] On June 22, France surrendered.

A view over the beach in Dunkirk in May 1940, as lines of Allied troops wait to be evacuated across the English Channel.

Preparing for Battle

Saving France from Hitler was no longer a possibility, but the United Kingdom had rescued a substantial fighting force from Dunkirk. Also, by refusing to give in to French requests for more air power, the United Kingdom had kept a significant part of the RAF intact.

Once Hitler realized that the British fully intended to continue to fight alone, he ordered a plan for the invasion of the United Kingdom to be drawn up. The code name for the proposed invasion was Operation Sea Lion. However, before German troops could cross the English Channel and land on the beaches of southern England, Hitler knew he needed to achieve dominance in the sky. As Churchill himself said in a speech on June 18, 1940: "The Battle of France is over. I expect that the Battle of Britain is about to begin."[1]

The Luftwaffe and the RAF

After the fall of France, there was a brief pause in the action, as both the Germans and the British reorganized and re-equipped. The Germans could now use airfields in northern France to launch their attacks on the United Kingdom. From the beginning of July 1940, the Luftwaffe began daily attacks on shipping in the English Channel. They used their "Stuka" dive-bombers to swoop down

RAF pilots of the Advanced Air Striking Force posing beside a Spitfire aircraft

Ministry of Aircraft Production

Churchill made an important decision when he put his old friend Lord Beaverbrook in charge of the Ministry of Aircraft Production. Beaverbrook was a wealthy newspaper owner and knew little about planes. His appointment was not a popular choice. Churchill's secretary described Beaverbrook as "twenty-five percent thug, fifteen percent crook, and the remainder a combination of genius and real goodness of heart."[4] But Churchill's choice was a good one. Beaverbrook had great energy and knew how to get results. Aircraft production increased and kept up with demand throughout the Battle of Britain.[5]

The need for metal to make planes was so great that Lord Beaverbrook launched a "Saucepans into Spitfires" campaign. Here members of the Women's Voluntary Service are collecting aluminum pots and pans on a cart for recycling.

on **convoys** of small boats carrying supplies (usually coal) to ports on the east coast of Britain. Dowding was forced to send fighter planes out to patrol the Channel and to defend the ships.[2]

Aside from the fights over the Channel, Dowding had many other matters on his mind. The RAF had lost around 500 fighter aircraft in the fight for France, and they needed to be replaced as fast as possible. Thanks to the Ministry of Aircraft Production (see the box above), fighter aircraft were quickly repaired or replaced.

Pilots, however, were more difficult to replace. Those who had survived the fighting in France had gained valuable combat experience. But in order to build up adequate numbers for the battle to come, pilots from many different countries were recruited into the RAF. They came from the occupied countries of Europe—Poland, Czechoslovakia, Belgium, and France—as well as from countries of the British Empire, including New Zealand, Canada, and Australia, in addition to a few volunteer pilots from the United States.[3]

The mood of the nation

The news that France had fallen and the United Kingdom must fight on alone prompted a variety of responses. Many people, including King George VI, were glad to be able to continue "fighting the war." In the United States, the official policy was one of neutrality, although there were shipments of weapons and armaments across the Atlantic to help replace some of the equipment abandoned at Dunkirk.

For many people in the United Kingdom, however, the prospect of fighting alone—and of possible invasion—was terrifying. Churchill knew that it was essential to make people believe that the country could survive, no matter how grim the reality of the situation.

One of his most potent weapons was his **oratory** skill—his ability to write and deliver stirring and powerful speeches at moments of great crisis. By speaking directly to the British people (often via the radio), Churchill was able to establish his policy of "no surrender" firmly in people's minds, and to make them feel that they were not alone in the fight against Hitler.

Practical matters

In addition to inspiring people with his oratory, Churchill knew that it was important to involve the whole nation—the "home front"—in the war effort. In May 1940, four days after Churchill became prime minister, Secretary of State for War Anthony Eden issued a call for men who were not eligible for military service to join the Local Defense Volunteers—a name Churchill changed in

Churchill's speeches

The speeches Churchill gave during World War II are some of the most famous ever spoken in the English language. He delivered some of them to MPs in the House of Commons, while others were broadcast on the radio. All over the country, people listened on their radio sets (there were no television broadcasts in the United Kingdom during the war).

You can hear a selection of Churchill's wartime speeches at: archive.org/details/Winston_Churchill and www.bbc.co.uk/history/worldwars/wwtwo/churchill_audio_01.shtml.

You can also read them at:
www.winstonchurchill.org/learn/speeches/speeches-of-winston-churchill.

Decisive words: "Their finest hour"

One of Churchill's best-known and most stirring speeches was given in the House of Commons, then broadcast on the radio, on June 18, 1940, when he said:

"The whole fury and might of the enemy must very soon be turned on us. Hitler knows that he will have to break us in this Island or lose the war. If we can stand up to him, all Europe may be free and the life of the world may move forward into broad, sunlit uplands. But if we fail, then the whole world, including the United States, including all that we have known and cared for, will sink into the abyss... Let us therefore brace ourselves to our duties, and so bear ourselves that, if the British Empire and its Commonwealth last for a thousand years, men will still say, 'This was their finest hour.'"[7]

May 13, 1940: Winston Churchill broadcasts the speech on the BBC that he had just delivered in the House of Commons: "I have nothing to offer but blood, toil, tears, and sweat..."

July 1940 to the catchier "Home Guard." The idea was to create a **civilian** "army" to help stop any invasion, and the response was overwhelming.

Churchill also introduced full-scale rationing (creating allowances or limits), not only of food, but also of items such as clothing and gasoline that were soon in short supply. The aim was fairness—a common standard of living to which everyone, no matter how rich or poor, would be held. The reality was the development of a thriving "black market," meaning a system of illegal trading for valuable items such as gasoline coupons, eggs, nylon stockings, and cigarettes.[6]

Fighter Command

By July 1940, there were 58 squadrons in Fighter Command, each one made up of around 12 fighter planes with 20 pilots at full strength. Under Dowding's direction, the squadrons were divided into four groups that covered all of the United Kingdom. One group, known as 13 Group, was responsible for the north of the United Kingdom, with its headquarters in Newcastle. The German occupation of Norway meant the Luftwaffe could launch attacks from there on targets in Scotland and the north of England. Another group, called 12 Group, covered the Midlands, and 10 Group covered Wales and the southwest of England.

The biggest group, however, was 11 Group, which covered London and the southeast of England. Air Vice-Marshal Keith Park was in charge of this group, which meant he had to organize the largest number of squadrons and airfields. Dowding knew that the major threat from the Luftwaffe came from the bases in occupied France, Holland, and Belgium, and that the biggest attacks would be around London—and so 11 Group would be critical to the RAF effort.

This map shows clearly why 11 Group in the southeast of England suffered the heaviest casualties and the most damage from Luftwaffe attacks during the Battle of Britain.

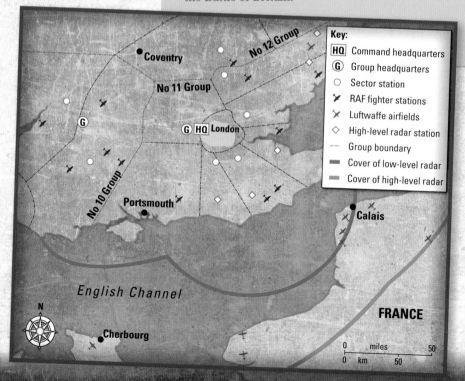

Key:
- **HQ** Command headquarters
- **G** Group headquarters
- ○ Sector station
- ✗ RAF fighter stations
- ✗ Luftwaffe airfields
- ◇ High-level radar station
- ---- Group boundary
- ▬ Cover of low-level radar
- ▬ Cover of high-level radar

Coventry

No 12 Group

No 11 Group

London

No 10 Group

Portsmouth

Calais

English Channel

N

FRANCE

Cherbourg

miles 0 — 50
km 0 — 50

Bentley Priory

Although all four groups had their own separate headquarters, the heart of Fighter Command was the operational center at a place called Bentley Priory. Here, Dowding was able to keep track of what was going on in the air once the Battle of Britain started.

Dowding and others were able to use the radar network he had set up before the war (see page 21), in addition to information provided by the men and women from a group called the Observer Corps. The routes of incoming enemy planes were plotted on a giant tabletop map in the operations room, while lights on a "tote board" lit up to show which UK squadrons were airborne in response to enemy planes. Telephone cables— laid deep underground, to protect them from bombing— allowed Dowding to keep in close contact with the four group headquarters, to share information and issue commands.[8]

Hugh Dowding 1882–1970

Born: Moffat, United Kingdom

Role: Head of Fighter Command

Hugh Dowding was largely responsible for the defeat of the Luftwaffe in the Battle of Britain. He had been a squadron commander in the Royal Flying Corps in World War I. As head of Fighter Command, in 1936 he pushed for the development of fighter planes (Spitfires and Hurricanes) and of radar, both of which proved crucial in the Battle of Britain.[10]

Did you know? Despite the central role played by Dowding in the Battle of Britain, he was not a popular figure in the high command of the RAF. In November 1940, he was forced to retire from his post as head of Fighter Command (see pages 46 and 47).

Game of chess

By July 1940, the Germans were trying to gauge the strength of the RAF by launching small-scale raids. Like a player in a chess game, Dowding deliberately kept down the numbers of fighters he sent out in response. He wanted to trick the German command into thinking that UK fighter strength was small. For his part, the head of the Luftwaffe, Hermann Goering, assumed that an all-out attack on UK airfields would quickly wipe out the threat from the RAF and allow Operation Sea Lion—the plan for the invasion of the United Kingdom (see page 30)—to begin.[9]

The French Navy

While the first skirmishes of the Battle of Britain were being fought during the early summer of 1940, Prime Minister Churchill had other difficult decisions to make. The fall of France had left the fate of the powerful French Navy undecided. The terms of the armistice between France and Germany had stated that the French fleet would be "demobilized and disarmed under German or Italian control."[11] But Churchill doubted that he could trust Hitler's word, and he was determined that the Germans should not have the use of the French warships.

Action at Oran

There were significant numbers of French ships in Alexandria, Egypt, at the eastern end of the Mediterranean, and at Mers-el-Kébir (Oran), in Algeria. In early July, Churchill sent orders to members of the Royal Navy in these areas to offer the French commanders options. These included sailing to a UK port or scuttling (sinking) their ships.

In Alexandria, Admiral Andrew Cunningham managed to negotiate a peaceful solution. But at Oran, Admiral James Somerville failed to come to terms with the French admiral. Following his orders from the UK government, Somerville eventually opened fire on the French ships, sinking one warship and damaging many others. Around 1,250 French sailors were killed in this action, and many hundreds more were injured.

Decisive words: Churchill to Admiral Somerville

This was the message Churchill sent to Admiral Somerville on July 2, 1940, instructing him to fire on the French fleet if necessary:

"You are charged with one of the most disagreeable and difficult tasks that a British Admiral has ever been faced with, but we have complete confidence in you and rely on you to carry it out relentlessly."[17]

"A terrible decision"

Churchill reported the action at Oran to the House of Commons on July 4, 1940. As he sat down at the end of his speech, he had tears running down his cheeks.[12]

He later wrote about Oran: "It was a terrible decision, like taking the life of one's own child to save the State."[13] But it delighted his fellow Conservatives, who cheered loudly. For the first time, Churchill had won approval from the majority of his own party.

The action at Oran soured relations between France and the United Kingdom for many years afterward. But it sent out a decisive message to the whole world about the United Kingdom's intentions.

Some in the German high command, including Hitler, still had hopes that Churchill's government would not survive, and that it would be replaced with one that was more inclined to negotiate peace with Germany. On July 19, in an address to the German parliament, Hitler offered the United Kingdom the choice between peace and "unending suffering and misery."[14] Churchill was unmoved. He told the House of Commons: "I don't propose to say anything in reply to Herr Hitler's speech, not being on speaking terms with him."[15]

Hitler had already set a date, August 15, for the invasion of the United Kingdom. But before then, it was up to Goering to neutralize the threat from the RAF.[16]

The Battle of Britain

The Luftwaffe's all-out attack on the RAF, code-named Eagle Day, was planned for August 10, but bad weather forced the Germans to postpone it. On August 12, the Luftwaffe bombed some of the radar stations that formed what was known as the Chain Home early warning system. The damage was limited, with only one station temporarily put out of action.

On August 13, the Luftwaffe switched its focus to the RAF's airfields and control centers on the ground. Most of these attacks were on 11 Group in southeast England, under the command of Air Vice-Marshal Park. In the month that followed, the planes, pilots, and aircrews of 11 Group suffered a terrible battering from the Luftwaffe bombers.

"The few"

On August 16, Churchill visited Park's 11 Group headquarters in Uxbridge. The fighting was intense, as hundreds of Luftwaffe bombers attacked airfields across southern England. As Churchill sat and watched the action, he was heard to mutter: "Never in the field of human combat has so much been owed by so many to so few." Four days later, he reused this phrase in a speech to the House of Commons. For many people, these words came to sum up the heroism shown by the pilots and crews of Fighter Command in the Battle of Britain.

Despite the damage and casualties inflicted by the Luftwaffe, both Dowding and Park resisted the temptation to pull the squadrons of 11 Group back north of the Thames River, as they knew that this was exactly what the Germans wanted. Emergency airfields were brought into action, where Spitfires and Hurricanes could take off from grass landing strips. But damage to facilities on the ground and casualties to ground crews meant that it was a huge challenge to keep aircraft in flying condition. Park called on backup from 10 Group and 12 Group to replace exhausted pilots and ground crews and to keep enough fighters in the air.

Big Wings

The fact that most of the action was being fought in the skies of 11 Group caused some resentment on the part of the commander in charge of 12 Group, Air Vice-Marshal Trafford Leigh-Mallory. Disagreement between Park and Leigh-Mallory led to a debate in Fighter Command over how many planes to fly.

The Luftwaffe usually operated in large groups of between 30 and 40 aircraft, whereas an RAF squadron was made up of around 12 fighter planes. As a result, the RAF pilots often found themselves outnumbered, but both Dowding and Park knew that sending in more fighters usually resulted in heavier losses. They preferred the flexibility and speed of intercepting the enemy with a small force, rather than trying to organize larger numbers of planes.

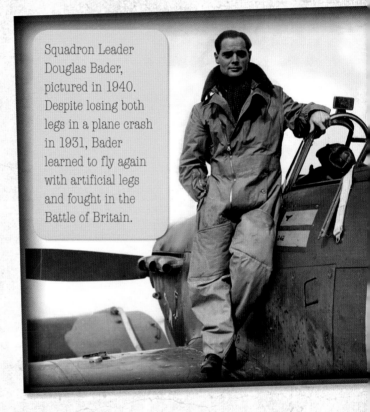

Squadron Leader Douglas Bader, pictured in 1940. Despite losing both legs in a plane crash in 1931, Bader learned to fly again with artificial legs and fought in the Battle of Britain.

Leigh-Mallory, however, promoted the "Big Wing" approach—meaning having three to five squadrons flying together in formation. The problem was that it took a lot of time for this number of squadrons to "scramble" (take off) and organize. On several occasions, when Park requested assistance from 12 Group, the Big Wing formations arrived at their target too late to be of any use.

However, Leigh-Mallory had the backing of one of the most colorful pilots in 12 Group, Squadron Leader Douglas Bader. The force of their arguments was to have a drastic outcome for both Park and Dowding before the end of 1940 (see pages 46 and 47).

Bombing blunder

The last week in August and the first week of September were a critical time in the Battle of Britain. During that time, the Luftwaffe sent up to 1,000 aircraft every day to try to bomb Fighter Command into submission. At airfields, the ground crews worked under constant attack, while the supply of trained pilots began to run dangerously short.

In order to keep up the pressure, the Germans also started nighttime bombing raids on cities. On the night of August 24–25, a navigational error led to German bombs being dropped on central London. This was against Goering's (and Hitler's) orders. In retaliation, Churchill ordered the RAF to bomb the German capital, Berlin.

RAF losses

The following numbers reflect the losses suffered by the RAF from August 24 to September 6, 1940:

- 295 Spitfires and Hurricanes lost
- 171 planes severely damaged
- 231 pilots killed or wounded.[1]

The actual damage inflicted by the RAF bombers on Berlin was minimal. But the damage to **morale** and Nazi pride was huge. Goering had promised the people of Berlin that the Luftwaffe would ensure their city would never be bombed, and he had boasted that the RAF was being "eliminated." The sound of air raid sirens and falling bombs therefore came as a considerable shock. Hitler's response was to announce a major bombing campaign against London. The raids started on September 7.

Summer, 1940: A squadron of German bombers fly in formation during an attack on England.

Turning point

Although it was far from clear at the time, many people now see this change of tactics as a turning point in the Battle of Britain. The accidental bombing of London in August had led to a new strategy being forced on the Luftwaffe. The Germans changed the focus of their bombing raids away from Fighter Command and on to cities and industries—particularly London. The Germans hoped to destroy public morale and the RAF in one final grand gesture. But the actual effect was to allow Fighter Command, which had come perilously close to exhaustion, a crucial breathing space in which to regroup.

Dowding knew that he could not prevent the Luftwaffe from dropping deadly bombs on London, but what he could do was ensure that losses of German aircraft and crews were so high that the bombing would eventually stop. Aircraft from all four Fighter Command groups responded to the German daylight raids on London that continued throughout September. But by September 11, more than 1,000 people in London had been killed in just four days.

Decisive words: "Hold firm"

On September 11, 1940, Churchill broadcast a speech to the people of London, saying:

The bombing of London by the Luftwaffe caused widespread damage and thousands of deaths. Winston Churchill knew the importance of keeping up public morale during the Blitz (see page 42).

"These cruel…indiscriminate [not specifically targeted] bombings of London are, of course, a part of Hitler's invasion plans. He hopes, by killing large numbers of civilians, and women and children, that he will terrorize and cow the people of this mighty imperial city… Little does he know the spirit of the British nation, or the tough fiber of the Londoners… This is a time for everyone to stand together, and hold firm, as they are doing."[2]

The Blitz

On the night of September 7, after the first day of the bombing of London, Air Vice-Marshal Park flew across London in his Hurricane and looked down on the scene of destruction below. He later remarked: "It was burning all down the River. It was a horrid sight. But I looked down and said, 'Thank God for that!' because I knew that the Nazis had now switched their attack from the Fighter Stations, thinking they were knocked out."[3]

The bombing, which became known as the Blitz, caused huge destruction, misery, and thousands of deaths and injuries in London. Churchill saw for himself the effects of the bombs—as well as the fires that devastated large parts of London—on his visits around the city to survey the damage. But despite the continuing raids, happening now both day and night, public morale remained unbroken.

The decisive day

Today, most historians agree that the climax of the Battle of Britain came on September 15, 1940, now known as Battle of Britain Day—although this was far from obvious at the time.

Night bombing

Back in June 1940, Churchill was alarmed by the accuracy of German nighttime bombing raids on industrial targets. The Air Ministry discovered that German pilots were using a system of radio beams to guide them through the darkness. Churchill knew that Fighter Command's ability to operate at night was extremely limited. Radar-equipped Blenheim night fighters were under development, but they were still in the experimental stage.

While it proved quite easy to block the first German system, by September 1940 the Germans already had a more sophisticated beam system in place. The race to figure out how this system worked, and how it could be jammed, continued throughout the fall of 1940. During this time, Luftwaffe bombing raids inflicted huge damage on cities such as Coventry, England. The inability of Fighter Command to prevent such nighttime raids was to be one of the factors that led to Dowding's downfall.[5]

The weekend of September 14–15 was widely predicted as "invasion weekend." Everyone was on high alert for the likely start of Operation Sea Lion, the Germans' plan to invade the United Kingdom. But Hitler wanted one more knockout blow from the Luftwaffe.

Waves of attacks on September 15 pushed the Fighter Command squadrons to their limits. The day ended, however, with heavy losses for the Luftwaffe. Hitler now knew that invasion was impossible. The RAF had not been neutralized, and the fall weather would soon make conditions in the Channel impossible for an attack by sea. Operation Sea Lion was postponed "indefinitely."[4]

On the UK side, the threat of invasion remained very real, and the autumn of 1940 was grim, as German bombing raids continued. The Luftwaffe ended most daylight raids by the beginning of October, because their losses were becoming too great. Instead, they mounted night raids on UK cities and industrial targets. The Blitz continued well into 1941.

Coventry lies in ruins after devastating bombing in November 1940.

After the Battle

In March 1941, the Air Ministry produced a booklet to commemorate the Battle of Britain. The booklet told the story of the heroic feats of the pilots and crews of Fighter Command who were pitted against the Luftwaffe. It ended, of course, in victory for the RAF and humiliation for the Luftwaffe.

The booklet was immensely popular and sold over 1 million copies in the United Kingdom.[1] Yet even as it was published, the Luftwaffe continued to bomb UK towns and cities. So, what was this victory? What did it mean for the British people? And what was Churchill's contribution?

What battle?

Some German historians argue that there was no short and decisive "Battle of Britain." They point out that the air campaign continued into 1941, and that the Luftwaffe remained operational and undefeated by the RAF. It is true that Fighter Command was unable to deliver a killer blow to the Luftwaffe. But simply by remaining in existence, and by preventing the Germans from gaining dominance in the air, the RAF achieved its aims: to make a German invasion of the United Kingdom impossible, and to protect the country from an all-out and crippling bombing offensive.

Hermann Goering (center), commander of the Luftwaffe, talks to two of his fighter pilots in October 1940. Goering promised Hitler that he would destroy the RAF, and lost considerable face when this did not happen.

Intelligence and tactics

The Germans failed to achieve their goals in 1940 largely because of poor intelligence (information) and a lack of coherent leadership. In fact, both the British and Germans had little accurate information about the strengths of each other's air forces, or about the numbers of planes lost each day (these were usually wildly overestimated).

Decisive words: "fruitless and aimless attacks"

Raymond Lee, a U.S. military expert in London, wrote these words on September 15, 1940:

"I can't for the life of me puzzle out what the Germans are up to. They have great air power and yet are dissipating it in fruitless and aimless attacks all over England. They must have an exaggerated idea of the damage they are doing and the effects of their raids on public morale."[4]

The Germans were also hampered by their head of Luftwaffe intelligence, Beppo Schmid, who was more concerned about pleasing Goering than about telling him the truth.[2] Schmid underestimated the strength and capabilities of the RAF, and he completely failed to take into account the effectiveness of Dowding's radar system. Goering similarly made wild promises to Hitler about what the Luftwaffe could achieve. His main tactical error, however, was a lack of clear strategy about what should be bombed and when. All too often, the Luftwaffe attacks did not concentrate on vital targets or follow up on successful raids.[3]

Churchill and Dowding

As Churchill later acknowledged, the successful outcome of the RAF's battle in 1940 was in a large part due to the leadership of Dowding. Dowding's early warning network and the communications systems set up at Bentley Priory (see page 35) were essential for success.

During the battle itself, Churchill put his trust in Dowding's considerable tactical skills. Dowding avoided sending large formations of aircraft to attack the Luftwaffe, preferring instead the flexibility and speed of scrambling squadrons of fighters to attack the German bombers. He knew that fighting big air battles would result in catastrophic losses for the RAF, and this theory was later proven correct. He also did not want the Germans to be able to calculate the true strength of Fighter Command, and in this he was also successful.

Dowding's "chicks"

Dowding was not the easiest man to get along with (his nickname was "Stuffy"), but he cared deeply about his fighter pilots, whom he sometimes referred to as "my chicks." When necessary, he was prepared to stand up to other officers in the RAF, the Air Ministry, and to Churchill himself. Dowding fought for and got bulletproof windshields for his fighter planes.[5] He also insisted that the phone lines connecting Bentley Priory to the other Fighter Command headquarters, and to the early warning network, should be buried deep underground and protected by concrete.

As the Battle of Britain raged in the skies above, Churchill was very interested in the progress of events, often visiting Dowding's or Park's headquarters to witness the drama of battle for himself. But he wisely left the day-to-day operations of Fighter Command to Dowding, Park, and the other RAF commanders.

Decisive words: "Support and confidence"

In 1941, Dowding wrote an account of the Battle of Britain. He began with these words:

"I trust that I may be permitted to record my appreciation of the help given me by the support and confidence of the prime minister at a difficult and critical time. In the early stages of the fight Mr. Winston Churchill spoke with affectionate raillery of me and my 'Chicks.' He could have said nothing to make me more proud; every Chick was needed before the end."[7]

This statue of Dowding stands outside St. Clement Danes Church in London. The inscription below the statue reads: "To him, the people of Britain and the Free World owe largely the way of life and the liberties they enjoy today."

Political intrigue

Many people believe that Dowding won the Battle of Britain. Yet both Dowding and Park lost their jobs as soon as the battle was over. In the fall of 1940, Leigh-Mallory and Bader claimed some success for the Big Wing theory (see page 39), although Park challenged these claims. At the same time, there was increasing concern about the slow development of effective night fighters under Dowding's command.

Churchill did not intervene in November 1940, when Dowding was forced into retirement. Park was also moved to a different role. Leigh-Mallory took over as commander of 11 Group, and later (in 1942) he became head of Fighter Command. Park wrote later: "To my dying day I shall feel bitter at the base intrigue which was used to remove Dowding and myself as soon as we had won the Battle of Britain."[6]

Why did Churchill not intervene to save Dowding? Some people think that Churchill never forgave Dowding for standing up to him over the issue of sending fighter squadrons to France (see page 27). Others point out that the air chief was due to retire back in 1939, and he was utterly exhausted after a summer and fall of intensive fighting. They argue that while Churchill's lack of support was harsh, it was also, given the circumstances, the correct decision.

Decisive words: "The art of war"

In his *History of the Second World War*, published in 1949, Churchill acknowledged Dowding's "genius," saying:

"The foresight of Air Marshal Dowding in his direction of Fighter Command deserves high praise, but even more remarkable had been the restraint and the exact measurement of formidable stresses which had reserved a fighter force in the North through all these long weeks of mortal conflict in the South. We must regard the generalship here shown as an example of genius in the art of war."[8]

New challenges

The Battle of Britain was a first defeat for Hitler in World War II, but it was still early in the war as a whole. With the home front secured for the time being, 1941 brought many other challenges for Churchill.

The United Kingdom relied on supplies of food and raw materials that were imported into the country by sea. At the outbreak of war, the two main tasks of the Royal Navy were therefore to defend the country from invasion and to protect merchant shipping on trade routes around the world.

The main German weapon in this battle was the submarine, or U-boat. At the start of the war, Germany had 57 U-boats in operation, but by July 1942 this fleet had increased to 300.[9] In defense against the U-boats, UK ships traveled in convoys with naval escorts. But Churchill admitted after the end of the war: "The only thing that really frightened me during the war was the U-boat peril."[10]

The United States

Once the immediate danger from invasion was over on the home front, the question for Churchill was what to do next. Churchill knew that he could not attack Germany's main forces in Europe, so he decided on a strategy of minor operations in North Africa and the Middle East. He believed that ongoing action was important for public morale.

Winston Churchill and President Franklin D. Roosevelt at a meeting in the White House, Washington, D.C., in June 1942. Churchill always considered the United States to be a vital ally.

Churchill also wanted to demonstrate to the Americans that the United Kingdom remained serious about fighting the war. Churchill was convinced that the only sure way of defeating Hitler was if the United States, with its huge manpower and industrial strength, entered the war. He had been in frequent communication with U.S. President Franklin D. Roosevelt since 1939, and by 1941 the United States was doing all it could, short of actually going to war, to aid the Allies.

But it was the Japanese attack in December 1941 on the U.S. naval base Pearl Harbor, Hawaii, that finally brought the United States into the war. Churchill later described his reaction to this news as one of absolute relief, saying: "No American will think it wrong of me if I proclaim that to have the United States at our side was to me the greatest joy."[11]

Decisive words: Help for the Soviet Union

Churchill made his position about the Soviet Union clear in a broadcast on the day of the German invasion, June 22, 1941, saying:

"No one has been a more consistent opponent of Communism than I have for the last twenty-five years. I will unsay no word that I have spoken about it. But all this fades away before the spectacle which is now unfolding… Any man or state who fights on against Nazidom will have our aid. Any man or state who marches with Hitler is our foe… It follows, therefore, that we shall give whatever help we can to Russia [the Soviet Union] and the Russian people."[12]

New ally

In June 1941, Hitler invaded the communist state of the **Soviet Union** (also called the USSR). Despite a lifelong dislike of **communism**, Churchill made it very clear that in the circumstances of the war, he would back anyone who was fighting the ultimate threat of Nazism. The United Kingdom and the Soviet Union became formal allies in June. However, a war-torn United Kingdom was able to offer very little practical assistance as the German armies moved into Soviet territory, although it did send convoys of armaments, at great cost to its merchant fleet and navy.

What if?

Many people have wondered what would have happened if the Battle of Britain had gone differently. What if Fighter Command had been unable to hold off the Luftwaffe? What if the German invasion of the United Kingdom had actually gone ahead?

The fact that the RAF existed to go into battle against the Luftwaffe was thanks in no small part to the vision and energy of Churchill. It was Churchill who appointed Hugh Trenchard to be chief of staff of the new RAF in 1919 (see pages 14 and 15), and it was Churchill's belief in the need for a strong air force that helped Trenchard to develop the RAF. In fact, some historians have argued that Churchill's focus on boosting the RAF in the mid-1930s led to the neglect of both the army and the navy. Others point out, however, that without Churchill's dogged insistence on building up the RAF, the Battle of Britain could very well have had a different outcome.

Would Hitler have invaded?

Historians have questioned how serious Hitler was about an invasion of the United Kingdom. After the fall of France in 1940, Hitler remained hopeful that both Churchill and the British people would realize the hopelessness of their situation. He was already considering a German offensive on a much bigger front in the East against the Soviet Union, and in many ways the continuing action in France was an unwelcome distraction.

Thinking the unthinkable

In the famous speech he gave to the House of Commons on June 4, 1940 (see page 29), Churchill presented a different vision of the future if the unthinkable happened and the United Kingdom was forced to surrender to the Nazis. He ended the speech with these words:

"If, which I do not for a moment believe, this Island or a large part of it were subjugated and starving, then our Empire beyond the seas, armed and guarded by the British Fleet, would carry on the struggle, until, in God's good time, the New World, with all its power and might, steps forth to the rescue and the liberation of the old."[13]

The reality was that the might of the Royal Navy and forces from the empire would have been unlikely to save the United Kingdom in the way Churchill described. Even then, Churchill knew only too well that his country's best hope was to survive, somehow, until the United States joined the war.

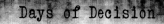

Goering reportedly assured Hitler that the Luftwaffe would quickly destroy the RAF, allowing an invasion to go ahead. Barges to transport troops and tanks were assembled in ports along the coasts of Belgium and Holland. The German plan of attack was for an overnight crossing to land troops on the south coast of England at dawn. But the Royal Navy had significant numbers of ships patrolling the Channel, and slow-moving German barges loaded with men and equipment would have been easy targets. Even if Hitler had given the go-ahead for invasion, would it have succeeded?

Adolf Hitler gives the Nazi salute to German Luftwaffe troops at a rally held in their honor in June 1939.

The proposed German invasion of Britain, code-named Operation Sea Lion, required large numbers of German troops to be transported across the English Channel.

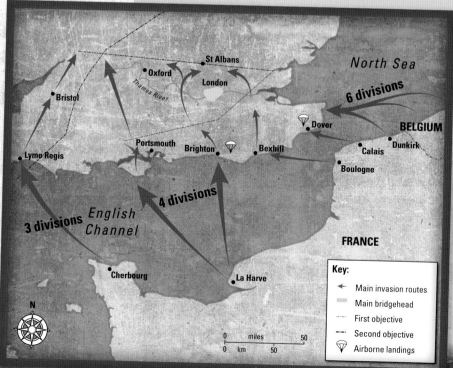

North Sea

St Albans
Oxford
London
Thames River
Bristol
6 divisions
BELGIUM
Dover
Portsmouth Brighton Bexhill
Dunkirk
Lyme Regis
Calais
Boulogne
4 divisions
English
3 divisions Channel
FRANCE
Cherbourg
La Harve

Key:
← Main invasion routes
▬ Main bridgehead
--- First objective
-·-· Second objective
▽ Airborne landings

N

0   miles   50
0   km   50

51

War leader

Looking back and knowing the outcome of the Battle of Britain and of World War II, it is easy to forget how uncertain and frightening the situation was for the United Kingdom after the fall of France in 1940. Many British people felt sure that a German invasion would come.

Churchill never attempted to hide from the British people how bad things were—for example, after the evacuation from Dunkirk, he was honest about the grim reality. But equally, he would not give up, and his speeches were an essential tool in making people believe that the United Kingdom could pull through. Churchill had real doubts about whether Hitler would, or practically could, mount an invasion of the United Kingdom.[14] He knew, however, that it was important to galvanize the nation into action and to ensure that every man and woman in the country felt that they were part of the war effort. Initiatives such as the Home Guard (see page 33) were all part of this strategy.

Churchill quickly stamped his authority on the country as a war leader. His experience in military matters, and particularly his long involvement with the RAF, was extremely valuable. No one else could match him for his energy and his oratory skill. Churchill was also one of the few people who had been unwavering in his assessment of Hitler and the dangers of Nazism in the years before the war. All of these elements made him an inspirational leader for the British people.

Winston Churchill gives the "V" for victory sign in June 1943. World War II finally came to an end on September 2, 1945.

He is not England?

On June 26, 1940, the minister of propaganda in Nazi Germany, Joseph Goebbels, wrote in his diary: "Are the English giving in? No sure signs visible yet. Churchill still talks big. But then he is not England."[15] In some respects, he was right in this assessment. At that time, there were many MPs, including fellow Conservatives, who did not support or trust Churchill. But as time went on, Churchill increasingly was "England"—he was the man who galvanized people into action and, most importantly, made the British people believe they could, and would, survive.

Writing history

After the war was over, Churchill wrote *The Second World War*, which was published from 1948 to 1953 in six volumes. As a personal account, the books are fascinating to read. At times, however, Churchill was careful to *rewrite* history to suit his own purposes. For example, we know that there were people in government who questioned Churchill's judgment in standing up to Hitler in 1940, yet in volume two, *Their Finest Hour*, Churchill wrote:

> "Future generations may deem it noteworthy that the supreme question of whether we should fight on alone never found a place upon the war cabinet agenda—we were much too busy to waste time upon such unreal, academic issues."[16]

Decisive words: "Perfectly suited"

Clem Attlee was a Labour politician who was deputy prime minister in Churchill's wartime coalition government. Writing after the war, he said:

> "Without Churchill, Britain might have been defeated. I do not say we would have been defeated. But we might have been. He was so perfectly suited to fulfil a particular need; the need was so vital; and the absence of anybody of his quality was so blatant that one cannot imagine what would have happened if he had not been there."[17]

53

Timeline

Winston Churchill's life up to World War II

1874
Winston Leonard Spencer Churchill is born on November 30

1894
Churchill graduates from the famous Royal Military Academy at Sandhurst

1895
Churchill travels to Cuba

1896
Churchill serves in India with the British Army

1925
Churchill returns to the Conservative Party

1924
Churchill becomes Chancellor of the Exchequer in the Conservative government

1921
Churchill moves to the Colonial Office

1918
Churchill becomes minister for war

1917
Churchill is back in government, as the minister for munitions

1929
Conservatives lose the general election; Churchill is out of office (until 1939)

1932
Churchill begins to speak out about the dangers of Hitler's Germany

1935
Churchill opposes the Government of India Act

1938
Prime Minister Neville Chamberlain meets Hitler in Munich; Churchill speaks out against the policy of appeasement

1940
September 15
Battle of Britain Day: Although the Blitz continues for many months to come, Hitler cancels his invasion plans, signaling the end of the Battle of Britain

1940
September 11
Churchill gives his "Hold Firm" speech

1940
September 7
Full-scale Luftwaffe raids begin on London

1940
August 24–25
Luftwaffe bombs fall on central London; the RAF retaliates with raids on Berlin

1899

Churchill leaves the British Army for a career in politics; he goes to South Africa as a war correspondent, where he is taken prisoner and escapes

1900

Churchill becomes Conservative MP for Oldham, England

1904

Churchill leaves the Conservatives and joins the opposition Liberal Party

1908

Churchill marries Clementine Hozier

1915

The Gallipoli campaign is fought (February–January 1916); Churchill loses his job and returns to the British Army

1914–1918

World War I is fought

1911

Churchill becomes first lord of the Admiralty

1910

Churchill is promoted to the role of home secretary

The Battle of Britain

1939

Churchill becomes first lord of the Admiralty upon the outbreak of World War II

1940

May 10
Chamberlain resigns; Churchill becomes prime minister

1940

May 27–June 4
Allied soldiers are evacuated from Dunkirk

1940

June 18
Churchill gives his "Their Finest Hour" speech, in which he warns of the "Battle of Britain" to come

1940

August 20
Churchill gives his "The Few" speech, celebrating the RAF

1940

August 12
"Eagle Day": The Luftwaffe begins its bombardment of Fighter Command

1940

July 10–August 11
Battles over the English Channel begin between the Luftwaffe and Fighter Command

1940

June 22
France surrenders

Notes on Sources

A Decisive Day
(pages 4–5)

1. James Holland, *The Battle of Britain* (London: Bantam Press, 2010), 567.

2. Max Hastings, *Finest Years: Churchill as Warlord, 1940–45* (London: HarperPress, 2009), 13.

3. *Ibid.*, xviii.

Who Was Winston Churchill?
(pages 6–9)

1. The Churchill Center and Museum, "Biography: Harrow School," http://www.winstonchurchill.org/learn/biography/the-child/harrow.

2. Richard Holmes, *In the Footsteps of Churchill* (London: BBC Books, 2005), 45.

3. The Churchill Center and Museum, "Speeches: The Maiden Speech," http://www.winstonchurchill.org/learn/speeches/speeches-of-winston-churchill/100-the-maiden-speech.

4. The Churchill Center and Museum, "Biography: War Correspondent," http://www.winstonchurchill.org/learn/biography/war-correspondent.

5. *Encyclopaedia Britannica*, "Sir Winston Churchill," http://www.britannica.com/EBchecked/topic/117269/Sir-Winston-Churchill.

6. Holmes, *In the Footsteps of Churchill*, 85.

7. Piers Brendon, "Sir Winston Churchill: Biographical History: The Family Man," Churchill Archives Center, Churchill College, Cambridge University, http://www.chu.cam.ac.uk/archives/collections/churchill_papers/biography/#FAMILY.

8. Mary Soames, *Winston and Clementine: The Personal Letters of the Churchills* (Boston: Houghton Mifflin, 2001), xiii.

Gallipoli and After
(pages 10–13)

1. Martin Gilbert, *Winston S. Churchill*, vol. 3 (*The Challenge of War, 1914–1916*) (Boston: Houghton Mifflin, 1971), 343.

2. Nigel Knight, *Churchill: The Greatest Briton Unmasked* (Cincinnati: David and Charles, 2008), 15.

3. *Ibid.*, 16.

4. Colin Nicolson, *Longman Companion to the First World War, 1914–1918* (New York: Longman, 2001), 121.

5. John Keegan, *The First World War* (London: Hutchinson, 1998), 268.

6. Gilbert, *Winston S. Churchill*, vol. 3, 429.

7. Nicolson, *Longman Companion to the First World War*, 123.

8. *Encyclopaedia Britannica*, "David Lloyd George," http://www.britannica.com/EBchecked/topic/345191/David-Lloyd-George.

Between Two Wars
(pages 14–23)

1. Royal Air Force, "RAF History: The Early Years of Military Flight," http://www.raf.mod.uk/history/shorthistoryoftheroyalairforce.cfm.

2. Martin Gilbert, "Churchill and Bombing Policy," The Churchill Center and Museum, http://www.winstonchurchill.org/images/pdfs/for_educators/Gilbert%20TCC%20Lecture%20CHURCHILL%20AND%20BOMBING%20POLICY.pdf.

3. Andrew Boyle, *Trenchard: Man of Vision* (London: Collins, 1962), #.

4. Holmes, *In the Footsteps of Churchill*, 138.

5. Richard M. Langworth, *Churchill's Wit* (London: Ebury Press, 2009), 75.

6. The National Archives, "The Cabinet Papers, 1915–1981: The Ten-Year Rule and Disarmament," http://www.nationalarchives.gov.uk/cabinetpapers/themes/10-year-rule-disarmament.htm.

7. Arthur Herman, *Gandhi and Churchill: The Epic Rivalry That Destroyed an Empire and Forged Our Age* (New York: Bantam, 2008), #.

8. Holmes, *In the Footsteps of Churchill*, 305.

9. Roy Jenkins, *Churchill* (London: Macmillan, 2001), 476.

10. Holmes, *In the Footsteps of Churchill*, 168.

11. Royal Air Force, "RAF History: The Inter-War Years, 1919–39," http://www.raf.mod.uk/history/shorthistoryoftheroyalairforce.cfm.

12. John Lake, *The Battle of Britain* (London: Amber Books, 2000), 13.

13. BBC History, "History: Historic Figures: Neville Chamberlain," http://www.bbc.co.uk/history/historic_figures/chamberlain_arthur_neville.shtml and *Encyclopaedia Britannica*, "Neville Chamberlain," http://www.britannica.com/EBchecked/topic/104904/Neville-Chamberlain.

14. Christopher Catherwood, *His Finest Hour* (London: Constable and Robinson, 2010), 126.

15. Nobel Prize, "The Nomination Database for the Nobel Prize in Peace, 1901–1956," http://www.nobelprize.org/nobel_prizes/peace/nomination/nomination.php?action=show&showid=2597.

16. The Churchill Center and Museum, "Speeches: The Munich Agreement," https://www.winstonchurchill.org/learn/speeches/speeches-of-winston-churchill/101-the-munich-agreement.

Outbreak of War
(pages 24–29)

1. Piers Brendon, "Sir Winston Churchill: Biographical History," Churchill Archives Center, Churchill College, Cambridge University, http://www.chu.cam.ac.uk/archives/collections/churchill_papers/biography and

Winston Churchill, *The Second World War*, vol. 1 (*The Gathering Storm*) (London: Cassell, 1948), 320.

2. Jenkins, *Churchill*, 584.

3. American Thinker, "I Felt As If I Were Walking With Destiny," http://www.americanthinker.com/2011/05/i_felt_as_if_i_were_walking_wi.html.

4. The Churchill Center and Museum, "Speeches: Blood, Toil, Tears and Sweat," https://www.winstonchurchill.org/learn/speeches/speeches-of-winston-churchill/92-blood-toil-tears-and-sweat.

5. Knight, *Churchill: The Greatest Briton Unmasked*, 116.

6. *Encyclopaedia Britannica*, "World War II," http://www.britannica.com/EBchecked/topic/648813/World-War-II#toc53531.

7. Royal Air Force, "The Second World War," http://www.raf.mod.uk/history/shorthistoryoftheroyalairforce.cfm.

8. Holland, *The Battle of Britain*, 159.

9. Jenkins, *Churchill*, 595.

10. Winston Churchill, *The Second World War*, vol. 2 (Their Finest Hour) (London: Cassell, 1948), 46.

11. Jenkins, *Churchill*, 619.

12. *Ibid.*, 597.

13. The Churchill Center and Museum, "Speeches: We Shall Fight on the Beaches," http://www.winstonchurchill.org/learn/speeches/speeches-of-winston-churchill/1940-finest-hour/128-we-shall-fight-on-the-beaches.

14. The Churchill Center and Museum, "Speeches: We Shall Fight on the Beaches," https://www.winstonchurchill.org/learn/speeches/speeches-of-winston-churchill/128-we-shall-fight-on-the-beaches.

Preparing for Battle (pages 30–37)

1. The Churchill Center and Museum, "Speeches: Their Finest Hour," https://www.winstonchurchill.org/learn/speeches/speeches-of-winston-churchill/122-their-finest-hour.

2. Michael Korda, *With Wings Like Eagles* (London: J. R. Books, 2009), 126.

3. Lake, *The Battle of Britain*, 86.

4. Kevin Jefferys, *The Churchill Coalition and Wartime Politics, 1940-1945* (New York: Manchester University Press, 1995), 37.

5. Korda, *With Wings Like Eagles*, 131.

6. History, "World War II," http://www.history.co.uk/explore-history/ww2.html.

7. The Churchill Center and Museum, "Speeches: Their Finest Hour."

8. Richard Overy, *The Battle of Britain Experience* (London: Carlton, 2010), 10.

9. Korda, *With Wings Like Eagles*, 157.

10. *Encyclopaedia Britannica*, "Hugh Caswall Tremenheere Dowding, 1st Baron Dowding," http://www.britannica.com/EBchecked/topic/170409/Hugh-Caswall-Tremenheere-Dowding-1st-Baron-Dowding.

11. Jenkins, *Churchill*, 622.

12. *Ibid.*, 625.

13. Hastings, *Finest Years*, 69.

14. World War II Multimedia Database, http://worldwar2database.com/gallery3/index.php/wwii0036.

15. Hastings, *Finest Years*, 78.

16. Korda, *With Wings Like Eagles*, 154.

17. Combined Operations, "Operation Catapult," http://www.combinedops.com/mers%20el%20kabir.htm.

The Battle of Britain (pages 38–43)

1. Royal Air Force, "The Second World War."

2. Teaching American History, "Winston Churchill: Every Man to His Post," http://teachingamericanhistory.org/library/index.asp?document=1911.

3. Battle of Britain Historical Society, "Saturday September 7th 1940," http://www.battleofbritain1940.net/0036.html.

4. Korda, *With Wings Like Eagles*, 281.

5. Len Deighton, *Battle of Britain* (London: Jonathan Cape, 1980), 196.

After the Battle (pages 44–53)

1. Overy, *The Battle of Britain Experience*, 80.

2. Holland, *The Battle of Britain*, 606.

3. Lake, *The Battle of Britain*, 42.

4. Deighton, *Battle of Britain*, 175.

5. Korda, *With Wings Like Eagles*, 38.

6. Lake, *The Battle of Britain*, 99.

7. The Spitfire Site, "Battle of Britain in the Words of Air Chief Marshal Hugh Dowding," http://spitfiresite.com/2010/04/battle-of-britain-in-the-words-of-air-chief-marshal-hugh-dowding.html.

8. Churchill, *The Second World War*, vol. 2, 286.

9. *Encyclopaedia Britannica*, "U-Boats," http://www.britannica.com/EBchecked/topic/612159/U-boat.

10. John Keegan, *The Second World War* (London: Pimlico, 1997), 83.

11. Winston Churchill, *The Second World War*, vol. 3 (The Grand Alliance) (London: Cassell, 1948), 539.

12. The Churchill Center and Museum, "Speeches: The Fourth Climacteric," https://www.winstonchurchill.org/learn/speeches/speeches-of-winston-churchill/809-the-fourth-climacteric.

13. The Churchill Center and Museum, "Speeches: We Shall Fight on the Beaches."

14. Hastings, *Finest Years*, 96.

15. *Ibid.*, 68.

16. New Statesman, "Every hero becomes a bore," http://www.newstatesman.com/books/2011/04/churchill-british-britain.

17. Holmes, *In the Footsteps of Churchill*, 206.

Glossary

Admiralty until 1964, government department in the UK responsible for the Royal Navy

Air Ministry from 1918 to 1964, government department in the UK responsible for the Royal Air Force

Allies in World War I, main members of the Allied forces were the British Empire, France, Russia, Italy, Japan and, later in the war, the United States. In World War II, main members of the Allied forces were France, Poland, and the British Empire, together with the Soviet Union and later the United States.

appeasement policy of conceding something to an aggressive power in order to keep the peace

armament weapon or other military supply necessary for war

armistice agreement between sides to stop fighting

artillery large guns, operated by gun crews, that fire missiles such as shells

blitzkrieg meaning "lightning war," German tactic used in World War II of fast-moving attacks by tanks and motorized artillery followed by troops, all well supported by air power

Boers also called Afrikaners, Dutch-speaking settlers of southern Africa during the 18th and 19th centuries

bombardment attack by artillery fire or bombing

bomber plane specially built to attack ground or sea targets by carrying and releasing bombs

British Expeditionary Force (BEF) force made up of troops from the UK and the British Empire, sent to fight on the European mainland in both World War I and World War II

casualty someone who is killed or injured in an accident or a war

Central Powers in World War I, the side fighting the Allies made up of Germany, Austria- Hungary, and the Ottoman Empire (Turkey)

Chancellor of the Exchequer in the UK government, the person who is responsible for all financial and economic matters

civilian person who is not a member of a country's armed forces

coalition government in the UK, a government in which political parties agree to work together

colonial refers to colonies— territories that are under the control of another country or state

communism system of government in which the state controls the economy and private ownership is abolished

Conservative Party center-right political party in the UK, emphasizing traditional values and customs

convoy group of vehicles that travel together for protection

demobilize process of returning troops to civilian life after the end of a conflict

dictator leader who holds absolute power

first lord of the Admiralty in the UK, the political (rather than military) head of the Royal Navy

free trade policy by a government of non-interference with imports and exports—for example, not imposing taxes on imports

general election in the UK parliamentary system, election in which everyone who is eligible votes for a member of Parliament to represent them in the House of Commons

Labour Party center-left political party in the UK, founded in 1900, forming the main opposition to the Conservative Party

Liberal Party center-left political party in the UK, that grew out of the Whig Party in 1859 and formed the main opposition to the Conservatives until the 1920s, when Labour took over as the main opposition before World War II

Luftwaffe German air force, set up in 1935

mine floating bomb that explodes if struck by an object such as a ship. Mines are also used on land, often laid together in an area, called a minefield.

morale belief and hope amongst a group of people, often in the face of adversity

Nazi Party National Socialist German Workers' Party, far-right, racist political party in Germany between 1920 and 1945

neutral not taking sides in a dispute between two sides

oratory type of public speaking that stirs and touches the listener

Ottoman Empire Turkish empire that lasted from 1299 until 1923

Parliament in the UK, body that governs the country, made up of the House of Commons and the House of Lords

prime minister head of an elected government

radar use of radio waves to detect the position, direction, and speed of objects (such as aircraft)

rearmament process of re-equipping with weapons

reconnaissance process of obtaining information, often about an enemy, by secretly inspecting or observing

Soviet Union single-party communist state that existed between 1922 and 1991. Also called the Union of Soviet Socialist Republics: USSR.

squadron in an air force, a unit of between 12 and 24 aircraft, usually of the same type of planes

torpedo self-propelled weapon that explodes when it hits its target

treaty formal agreement

U-boat German submarine

Find Out More

Books

Nonfiction

Bungay, Stephen. *The Most Dangerous Enemy: An Illustrated History of the Battle of Britain*. Minneapolis: Zenith, 2010.

Catherwood, Christopher. *His Finest Hour*. New York: Skyhorse, 2010.

Moore, Kate. *The Battle of Britain*. Long Island City, N.Y.: Osprey, 2010.

Overy, R. J. *The Battle of Britain: The Myth and Its Reality*. New York: W. W. Norton, 2001.

Web sites

www.battleofbritain1940.net
Visit the web site of the Battle of Britain Historical Society.

www.bbc.co.uk/history/battle_of_britain
This web site allows you to explore the Battle of Britain through clips from BBC programs.

www.bbm.org.uk/about.htm
Learn more about the Battle of Britain Monument in London.

www.chu.cam.ac.uk/archives/collections/churchill_papers
The Churchill Papers are located at Churchill College, at Cambridge University in England. The papers contain everything from Churchill's childhood letters and school reports to his final writings. They include his personal correspondence with friends and family and his official exchanges with kings, presidents, politicians, and military leaders.

www.nationalarchives.gov.uk/cabinetpapers/themes/total-war.htm?WT.ac=Total%20war
The UK National Archive web site allows you to search important documents from the world wars by theme.

www.raf.mod.uk/history/battleofbritain70thanniversary.cfm
This RAF web site remembers the 70th anniversary of the Battle of Britain (in 2010).

www.winstonchurchill.org
Visit the web site of the Churchill Centre and Museum in London.

Other topics to research

Do research to learn more about topics related to the book. The following are some ideas to get you started:

- The Blitz: How did the people of London survive months of almost continuous bombing from the fall of 1940 to the spring of 1941?

- Douglas Bader: Bader was the squadron leader in Fighter Command 12 Group. He had led an eventful life even before flying in the Battle of Britain. In 1931, he lost both legs in a flying accident, yet he persuaded the RAF to let him fly in the war and ended up as a prisoner of war in the infamous Colditz Castle.

- Hugh Dowding and Fighter Command: Read more about Dowding and his "chicks." Find out more about Chain Home and the Observer Corps, as well as the men who took to the skies during the Battle of Britain. Learn also about the women pilots who ferried aircraft (although they were not involved in combat).

- Churchill and World War II: What happened after the Battle of Britain? Examine Churchill's relationships with U.S President Franklin D. Roosevelt and Soviet leader Joseph Stalin, as well as the eventual return of UK troops to France in the D-Day landings.

Index